Happy Easter to

_______________________.

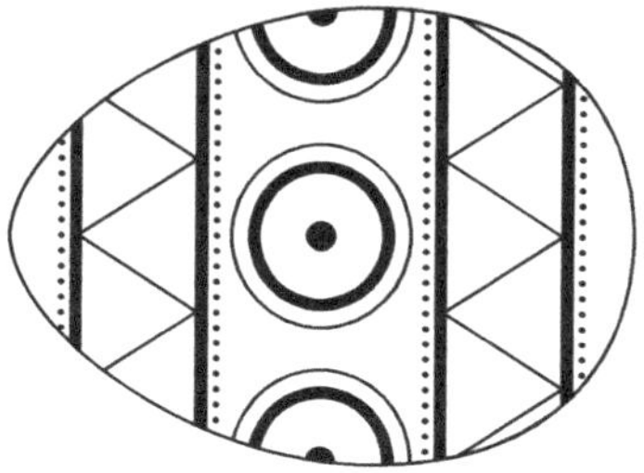

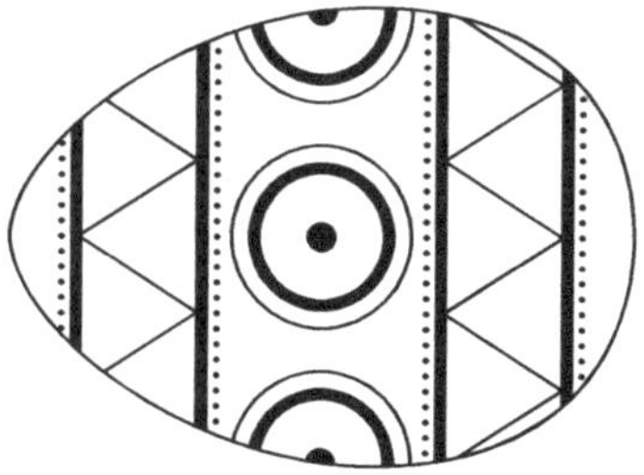

Grandma & Me Easter Coloring Book

Color With Me!

Sandy Mahony
Mary Lou Brown

smile
eggs
Happy
Easter
sun
love
HAPPY
EGG
life
bunny
joy
good
chicken
spring

Happy Easter

www.ingramcontent.com/pod-product-compliance
Lightning Source LLC
Chambersburg PA
CBHW081412280526
45788CB00009B/3077
9781542709477